THIS PLANNER BELONGS TO

____

____

____

Hey there, Superstar!

Welcome to your very own ADHD Planner – the ultimate tool to help you stay organized, focused, and ready to conquer each day! This planner is here to make planning fun and easy, guiding you step-by-step through your tasks and helping you shine brighter in everything you do.

Get ready to break down big tasks into small, achievable steps, set goals, and celebrate all your amazing progress. Remember, every big goal starts with one small step – and you've got everything it takes to make it happen!

Let's dive in and make every day a win!

AGE:

BIRTHDAY:

MY FAVORITE

FOOD:

COLOR:

PET:

MOVIE:

SPORT:

SUBJECT:

HOLIDAY:

NAME:

FUN FACTS ABOUT ME ...

WHEN I GROW UP I WANT TO BE ...

EMERGENCY CONTACT INFORMATION

Child's Name:

Date of Birth: Age:

Parent/Guardian 1

| Name: |
| Relationship: |
| Phone (Primary): |
| Phone (Secondary): |
| Email: |
| Address: |

Parent/Guardian 2 (if applicable):

| Name: |
| Relationship: |
| Phone (Primary): |
| Phone (Secondary): |
| Email: |
| Address: |

Important Notes or Medical Information:

MY SCHOOL CONTACT

School Name _______________________________

Teacher's Name:	
Teacher's Email:	
Teacher's Phone:	

School Counselor:	
Counselor's Email:	
Counselor's Phone:	

Special Ed Coordinator's Name:	
Counselor's Email:	
Counselor's Phone:	

Main Office Phone:	
Main Office Email:	

JANUARY

M	T	W	T	F	S	S
			1	2	3	4
5	6	7	8	9	10	11
12	13	14	15	16	17	18
19	20	21	22	23	24	25
26	27	28	29	30	31	

FEBRUARY

M	T	W	T	F	S	S
						1
2	3	4	5	6	7	8
9	10	11	12	13	14	15
16	17	18	19	20	21	22
23	24	25	26	27	28	

MARCH

M	T	W	T	F	S	S
						1
2	3	4	5	6	7	8
9	10	11	12	13	14	15
16	17	18	19	20	21	22
23	24	25	26	27	28	29
30	31					

APRIL

M	T	W	T	F	S	S
		1	2	3	4	5
6	7	8	9	10	11	12
13	14	15	16	17	18	19
20	21	22	23	24	25	26
27	28	29	30			

MAY

M	T	W	T	F	S	S
				1	2	3
4	5	6	7	8	9	10
11	12	13	14	15	16	17
18	19	20	21	22	23	24
25	26	27	28	29	30	31

JUNE

M	T	W	T	F	S	S
1	2	3	4	5	6	7
8	9	10	11	12	13	14
15	16	17	18	19	20	21
22	23	24	25	26	27	28
29	30					

JULY

M	T	W	T	F	S	S
		1	2	3	4	5
6	7	8	9	10	11	12
13	14	15	16	17	18	19
20	21	22	23	24	25	26
27	28	29	30	31		

AUGUST

M	T	W	T	F	S	S
					1	2
3	4	5	6	7	8	9
10	11	12	13	14	15	16
17	18	19	20	21	22	23
24	25	26	27	28	29	30
31						

SEPTEMBER

M	T	W	T	F	S	S
	1	2	3	4	5	6
7	8	9	10	11	12	13
14	15	16	17	18	19	20
21	22	23	24	25	26	27
28	29	30				

OCTOBER

M	T	W	T	F	S	S
			1	2	3	4
5	6	7	8	9	10	11
12	13	14	15	16	17	18
19	20	21	22	23	24	25
26	27	28	29	30	31	

NOVEMBER

M	T	W	T	F	S	S
						1
2	3	4	5	6	7	8
9	10	11	12	13	14	15
16	17	18	19	20	21	22
23	24	25	26	27	28	29
30						

DECEMBER

M	T	W	T	F	S	S
	1	2	3	4	5	6
7	8	9	10	11	12	13
14	15	16	17	18	19	20
21	22	23	24	25	26	27
28	29	30	31			

2026 HOLIDAYS

DATE	HOLIDAYS
Jan 1	New Year's Day
Jan 15	Martin Luther King Jr. Day
Feb 14	Valentine's Day
Feb 19	Presidents' Day
Mar 17	St. Patrick's Day
Apr 20	Easter Sunday
Apr 21	Easter Monday
Apr 15	Tax Day
May 5	Cinco de Mayo
May 12	Mother's Day
May 27	Memorial Day
Jun 14	Flag Day
Jun 16	Father's Day
Jun 19	Juneteenth
July 4	Independence Day
Sep 2	Labor Day
Oct 14	Columbus Day
Oct 31	Halloween
Nov 5	Election Day
Nov 11	Veterans Day
Nov 28	Thanksgiving Day
Nov 29	Black Friday
Dec 25	Christmas Day

BIRTHDAY TRACKER

January	February	March

April	May	June

July	August	September

October	November	December

IMPORTANT DATES

January	February	March

April	May	June

July	August	September

October	November	December

DAILY ROUTINE

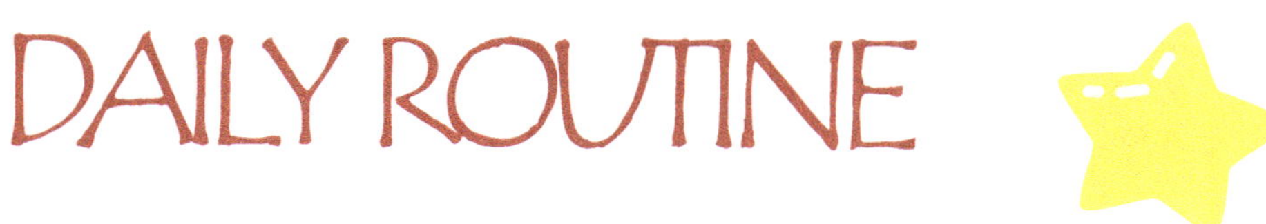

In The Morning

In The Afternoon

In The Evening

DAILY CHECKLIST

- Wake up early
- Brush Teeth
- Brush Hair
- Make a bed
- Get Dressed
- Clean Room
- Finish Homework
- Feed / Water pet
- Empty Dishwasher
- Take a nap

WEEKLY ROUTINE

WEEK: _________________

ROUTINE	Mon	Tue	Wed	Thu	Fri	Sat	Sun
	☐	☐		☐	☐	☐	☐
	☐	☐		☐	☐	☐	☐
	☐	☐		☐	☐	☐	☐
	☐	☐		☐	☐	☐	☐
	☐	☐		☐	☐	☐	☐
	☐	☐		☐	☐	☐	☐
	☐	☐		☐	☐	☐	☐
	☐	☐		☐	☐	☐	☐
	☐	☐		☐	☐	☐	☐
	☐	☐		☐	☐	☐	☐
	☐	☐		☐	☐	☐	☐
	☐	☐		☐	☐	☐	☐
	☐	☐		☐	☐	☐	☐
	☐	☐		☐	☐	☐	☐
	☐	☐		☐	☐	☐	☐
	☐	☐		☐	☐	☐	☐

MONTHLY ROUTINE

DAILY SCHEDULE

SCHEDULE	TO-DO
6:00	
7:00	
8:00	
9:00	
10:00	
11:00	
12:00	
13:00	
14:00	
15:00	
16:00	
17:00	
18:00	
19:00	
20:00	
21:00	
22:00	
23:00	
24:00	

WEEKLY SCHEDULE

Monday

Tuesday

Wednesday

Thursday

Friday

Saturday

Sunday

DAILY CHECKLIST

Starting Date	Ending Date	Details

Notes

WEEKLY SCHEDULE

Goals For   The Week

Tasks To Accomplish

This Week's Priorities

WEEKLY GRATITUDE

Affirmations

Highlight Of The Week

MONDAY

Date:

Daily Schedule

| 6:00 AM |
| 7:00 AM |
| 8:00 AM |
| 9:00 AM |
| 10:00 AM |
| 11:00 AM |
| 12:00 AM |
| 1:00 PM |
| 2:00 PM |
| 3:00 PM |
| 4:00 PM |
| 5:00 PM |
| 6:00 PM |
| 7:00 PM |
| 8:00 PM |
| 9:00 PM |
| 10:00 PM |
| 11:00 PM |
| 12:00 PM |

Mood

Weather

Water

Meal

Breakfast:

Lunch:

Dinner:

To-Do

Notes

TUESDAY

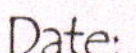

Daily Schedule

| 6:00 AM |
| 7:00 AM |
| 8:00 AM |
| 9:00 AM |
| 10:00 AM |
| 11:00 AM |
| 12:00 AM |
| 1:00 PM |
| 2:00 PM |
| 3:00 PM |
| 4:00 PM |
| 5:00 PM |
| 6:00 PM |
| 7:00 PM |
| 8:00 PM |
| 9:00 PM |
| 10:00 PM |
| 11:00 PM |
| 12:00 PM |

Mood

Weather

Water

Meal

Breakfast:

Lunch:

Dinner:

To-Do

Notes

WEDNESDAY

Date:

Daily Schedule

6:00 AM
7:00 AM
8:00 AM
9:00 AM
10:00 AM
11:00 AM
12:00 AM
1:00 PM
2:00 PM
3:00 PM
4:00 PM
5:00 PM
6:00 PM
7:00 PM
8:00 PM
9:00 PM
10:00 PM
11:00 PM
12:00 PM

Mood

Weather

Water

Meal

Breakfast:

Lunch:

Dinner:

To-Do

Notes

THURSDAY

Date:

Daily Schedule

6:00 AM
7:00 AM
8:00 AM
9:00 AM
10:00 AM
11:00 AM
12:00 AM
1:00 PM
2:00 PM
3:00 PM
4:00 PM
5:00 PM
6:00 PM
7:00 PM
8:00 PM
9:00 PM
10:00 PM
11:00 PM
12:00 PM

Mood

Weather

Water

Meal

Breakfast:

Lunch:

Dinner:

To-Do

Notes

FRIDAY

Date:

Daily Schedule

| 6:00 AM |
| 7:00 AM |
| 8:00 AM |
| 9:00 AM |
| 10:00 AM |
| 11:00 AM |
| 12:00 AM |
| 1:00 PM |
| 2:00 PM |
| 3:00 PM |
| 4:00 PM |
| 5:00 PM |
| 6:00 PM |
| 7:00 PM |
| 8:00 PM |
| 9:00 PM |
| 10:00 PM |
| 11:00 PM |
| 12:00 PM |

Mood

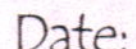

Weather

Water

Meal

Breakfast:

Lunch:

Dinner:

To-Do

Notes

SATURDAY

Daily Schedule

6:00 AM	
7:00 AM	
8:00 AM	
9:00 AM	
10:00 AM	
11:00 AM	
12:00 AM	
1:00 PM	
2:00 PM	
3:00 PM	
4:00 PM	
5:00 PM	
6:00 PM	
7:00 PM	
8:00 PM	
9:00 PM	
10:00 PM	
11:00 PM	
12:00 PM	

Mood

Weather

Water

Meal

Breakfast:

Lunch:

Dinner:

To-Do

Notes

SUNDAY

Daily Schedule

6:00 AM
7:00 AM
8:00 AM
9:00 AM
10:00 AM
11:00 AM
12:00 AM
1:00 PM
2:00 PM
3:00 PM
4:00 PM
5:00 PM
6:00 PM
7:00 PM
8:00 PM
9:00 PM
10:00 PM
11:00 PM
12:00 PM

Mood

Weather

Water

Meal

Breakfast:

Lunch:

Dinner:

To-Do

Notes

MY WEEK AT A GLANCE

Monday	Tuesday	Wednesday	Thursday	Friday	Saturday	Sunday

JANUARY  2026

Monday	Tuesday	Wednesday	Thursday	Friday	Saturday	Sunday
			1	2	3	4
5	6	7	8	9	10	11
12	13	14	15	16	17	18
19	20	21	22	23	24	25
26	27	28	29	30	31	

MONTHLY TASK & APPOINTMENTS

- ○ __________________________
- ○ __________________________
- ○ __________________________
- ○ __________________________
- ○ __________________________
- ○ __________________________
- ○ __________________________
- ○ __________________________
- ○ __________________________

MONTHLY GOALS

- ○ __________________________
- ○ __________________________
- ○ __________________________
- ○ __________________________
- ○ __________________________
- ○ __________________________
- ○ __________________________
- ○ __________________________
- ○ __________________________

FEBRUARY

2026

Monday	Tuesday	Wednesday	Thursday	Friday	Saturday	Sunday
						1
2	3	4	5	6	7	8
9	10	11	12	13	14	15
16	17	18	19	20	21	22
23	24	25	26	27	28	

MONTHLY TASK & APPOINTMENTS

○ ______________________________
○ ______________________________
○ ______________________________
○ ______________________________
○ ______________________________
○ ______________________________
○ ______________________________
○ ______________________________
○ ______________________________

MONTHLY GOALS

○ ______________________________
○ ______________________________
○ ______________________________
○ ______________________________
○ ______________________________
○ ______________________________
○ ______________________________
○ ______________________________
○ ______________________________

MARCH 2026

Monday	Tuesday	Wednesday	Thursday	Friday	Saturday	Sunday
						1
2	3	4	5	6	7	8
9	10	11	12	13	14	15
16	17	18	19	20	21	22
23	24	25	26	27	28	29
30	31					

MONTHLY TASK & APPOINTMENTS

○ ___________________________
○ ___________________________
○ ___________________________
○ ___________________________
○ ___________________________
○ ___________________________
○ ___________________________
○ ___________________________

MONTHLY GOALS

○ ___________________________
○ ___________________________
○ ___________________________
○ ___________________________
○ ___________________________
○ ___________________________
○ ___________________________
○ ___________________________

APRIL 2026

Monday	Tuesday	Wednesday	Thursday	Friday	Saturday	Sunday
		1	2	3	4	5
6	7	8	9	10	11	12
13	14	15	16	17	18	19
20	21	22	23	24	25	26
27	28	29	30			

MONTHLY TASK & APPOINTMENTS

- ○ ______________________________
- ○ ______________________________
- ○ ______________________________
- ○ ______________________________
- ○ ______________________________
- ○ ______________________________
- ○ ______________________________
- ○ ______________________________
- ○ ______________________________

MONTHLY GOALS

- ○ ______________________________
- ○ ______________________________
- ○ ______________________________
- ○ ______________________________
- ○ ______________________________
- ○ ______________________________
- ○ ______________________________
- ○ ______________________________
- ○ ______________________________

MAY  2026

Monday	Tuesday	Wednesday	Thursday	Friday	Saturday	Sunday
				1	2	3
4	5	6	7	8	9	10
11	12	13	14	15	16	17
18	19	20	21	22	23	24
25	26	27	28	29	30	31

MONTHLY TASK & APPOINTMENTS

- ○ ______________________________
- ○ ______________________________
- ○ ______________________________
- ○ ______________________________
- ○ ______________________________
- ○ ______________________________
- ○ ______________________________
- ○ ______________________________
- ○ ______________________________

MONTHLY GOALS

- ○ ______________________________
- ○ ______________________________
- ○ ______________________________
- ○ ______________________________
- ○ ______________________________
- ○ ______________________________
- ○ ______________________________
- ○ ______________________________
- ○ ______________________________

JUNE 2026

Monday	Tuesday	Wednesday	Thursday	Friday	Saturday	Sunday
1	2	3	4	5	6	7
8	9	10	11	12	13	14
15	16	17	18	19	20	21
22	23	24	25	26	27	28
29	30					

MONTHLY TASK & APPOINTMENTS

- ○ ______________________________
- ○ ______________________________
- ○ ______________________________
- ○ ______________________________
- ○ ______________________________
- ○ ______________________________
- ○ ______________________________
- ○ ______________________________

MONTHLY GOALS

- ○ ______________________________
- ○ ______________________________
- ○ ______________________________
- ○ ______________________________
- ○ ______________________________
- ○ ______________________________
- ○ ______________________________
- ○ ______________________________

JULY

2026

Monday	Tuesday	Wednesday	Thursday	Friday	Saturday	Sunday
		1	2	3	4	5
6	7	8	9	10	11	12
13	14	15	16	17	18	19
20	21	22	23	24	25	26
27	28	29	30	31		

MONTHLY TASK & APPOINTMENTS

- ○ ________________________
- ○ ________________________
- ○ ________________________
- ○ ________________________
- ○ ________________________
- ○ ________________________
- ○ ________________________
- ○ ________________________
- ○ ________________________

MONTHLY GOALS

- ○ ________________________
- ○ ________________________
- ○ ________________________
- ○ ________________________
- ○ ________________________
- ○ ________________________
- ○ ________________________
- ○ ________________________
- ○ ________________________

AUGUST  2026

Monday	Tuesday	Wednesday	Thursday	Friday	Saturday	Sunday
					1	2
3	4	5	6	7	8	9
10	11	12	13	14	15	16
17	18	19	20	21	22	23
24	25	26	27	28	29	30
31						

MONTHLY TASK & APPOINTMENTS

- ○ _______________________________
- ○ _______________________________
- ○ _______________________________
- ○ _______________________________
- ○ _______________________________
- ○ _______________________________
- ○ _______________________________
- ○ _______________________________
- ○ _______________________________

MONTHLY GOALS

- ○ _______________________________
- ○ _______________________________
- ○ _______________________________
- ○ _______________________________
- ○ _______________________________
- ○ _______________________________
- ○ _______________________________
- ○ _______________________________
- ○ _______________________________

SEPTEMBER  2026

Monday	Tuesday	Wednesday	Thursday	Friday	Saturday	Sunday
	1	2	3	4	5	6
7	8	9	10	11	12	13
14	15	16	17	18	19	20
21	22	23	24	25	26	27
28	29	30				

MONTHLY TASK & APPOINTMENTS

- ○ __________________________________
- ○ __________________________________
- ○ __________________________________
- ○ __________________________________
- ○ __________________________________
- ○ __________________________________
- ○ __________________________________
- ○ __________________________________
- ○ __________________________________
- ○ __________________________________

MONTHLY GOALS

- ○ __________________________________
- ○ __________________________________
- ○ __________________________________
- ○ __________________________________
- ○ __________________________________
- ○ __________________________________
- ○ __________________________________
- ○ __________________________________
- ○ __________________________________
- ○ __________________________________

OCTOBER 2026

Monday	Tuesday	Wednesday	Thursday	Friday	Saturday	Sunday
			1	2	3	4
5	6	7	8	9	10	11
12	13	14	15	16	17	18
19	20	21	22	23	24	25
26	27	28	29	30	31	

MONTHLY TASK & APPOINTMENTS

- ○ _______________________________
- ○ _______________________________
- ○ _______________________________
- ○ _______________________________
- ○ _______________________________
- ○ _______________________________
- ○ _______________________________
- ○ _______________________________
- ○ _______________________________

MONTHLY GOALS

- ○ _______________________________
- ○ _______________________________
- ○ _______________________________
- ○ _______________________________
- ○ _______________________________
- ○ _______________________________
- ○ _______________________________
- ○ _______________________________
- ○ _______________________________

NOVEMBER  2026

Monday	Tuesday	Wednesday	Thursday	Friday	Saturday	Sunday
						1
2	3	4	5	6	7	8
9	10	11	12	13	14	15
16	17	18	19	20	21	22
23	24	25	26	27	28	29
30						

MONTHLY TASK & APPOINTMENTS

- ○ ___________________________
- ○ ___________________________
- ○ ___________________________
- ○ ___________________________
- ○ ___________________________
- ○ ___________________________
- ○ ___________________________
- ○ ___________________________
- ○ ___________________________

MONTHLY GOALS

- ○ ___________________________
- ○ ___________________________
- ○ ___________________________
- ○ ___________________________
- ○ ___________________________
- ○ ___________________________
- ○ ___________________________
- ○ ___________________________
- ○ ___________________________

DECEMBER 2026

Monday	Tuesday	Wednesday	Thursday	Friday	Saturday	Sunday
	1	2	3	4	5	6
7	8	9	10	11	12	13
14	15	16	17	18	19	20
21	22	23	24	25	26	27
28	39	30	31			

MONTHLY TASK & APPOINTMENTS

- ○ _______________________
- ○ _______________________
- ○ _______________________
- ○ _______________________
- ○ _______________________
- ○ _______________________
- ○ _______________________
- ○ _______________________
- ○ _______________________

MONTHLY GOALS

- ○ _______________________
- ○ _______________________
- ○ _______________________
- ○ _______________________
- ○ _______________________
- ○ _______________________
- ○ _______________________
- ○ _______________________
- ○ _______________________

YEARLY PLANNER

January	**February**	**March**
April	**May**	**June**
July	**August**	**September**
October	**November**	**December**

THINGS TO DO

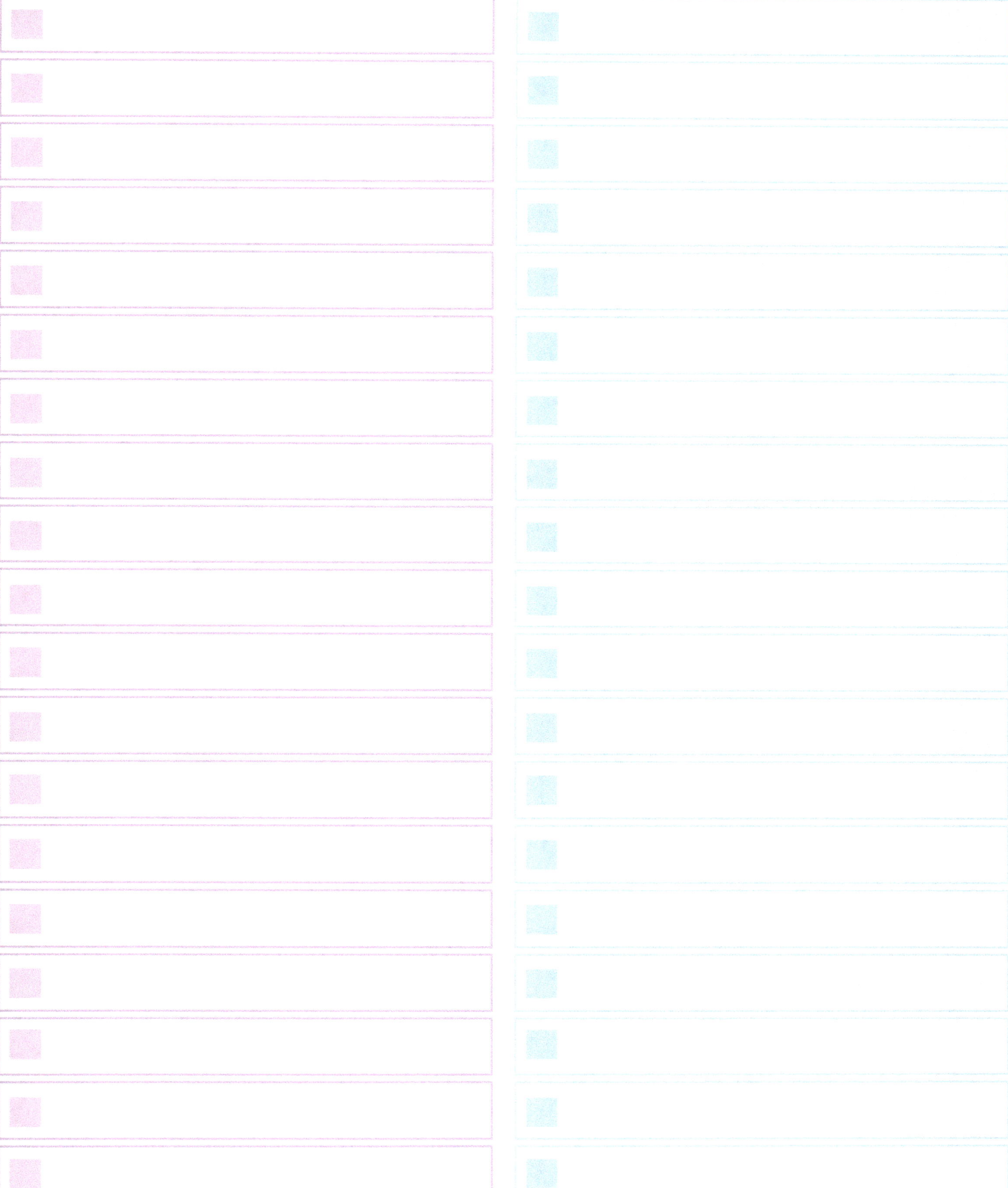

POSITIVE AFFIRMATIONS

I Believe in myself

I Deserve to be happy

I am good enough

I can achieve anything i want

I Believe in myself

MOOD TRACKER

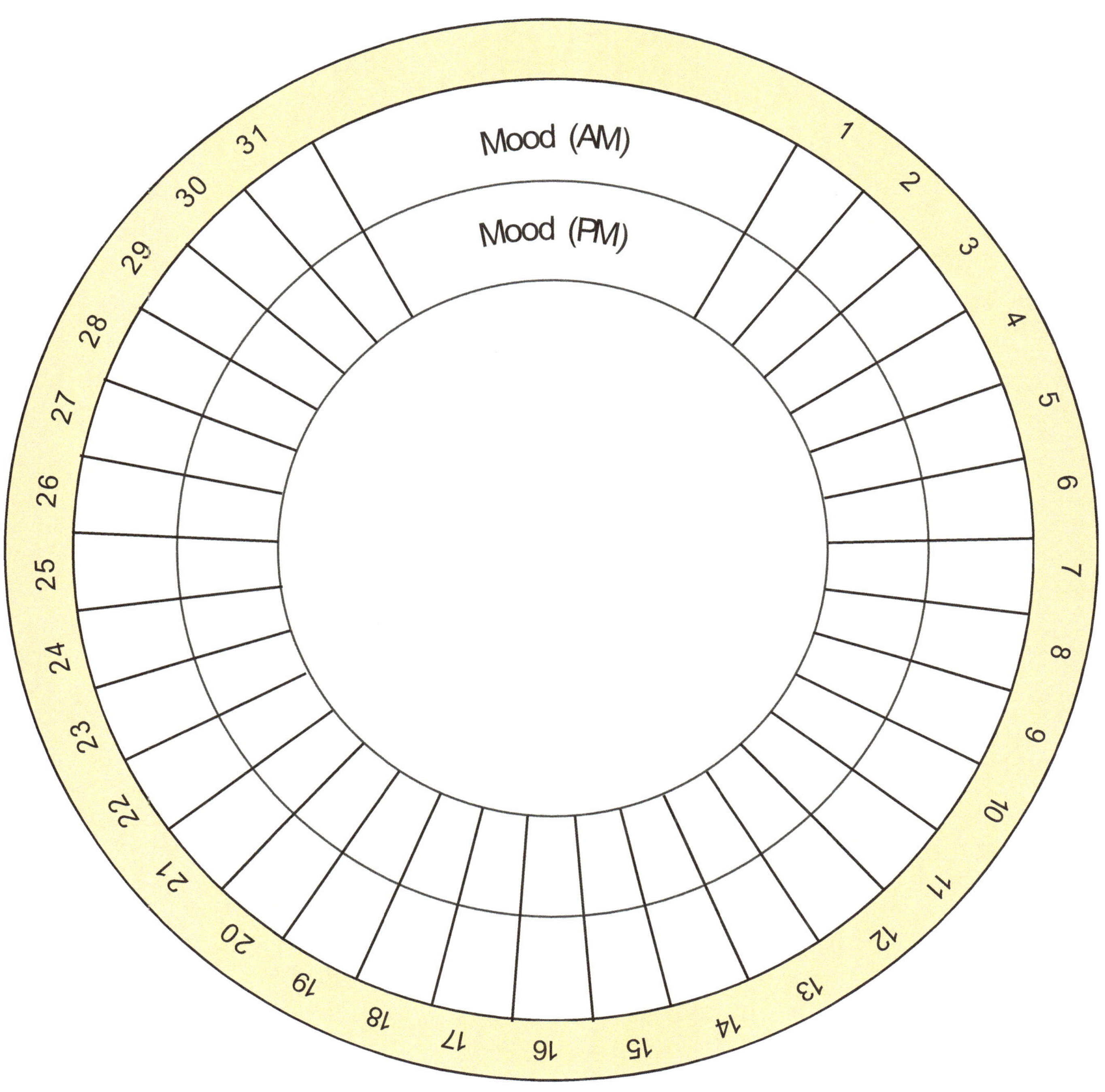

KEY

	Happy			Angry			Satisfied
	Sad			Excited			Confused

MOOD TRACKER

 =   = 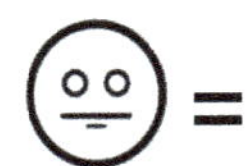 =  =

MOOD PIXEL IN A YEAR

	J	F	M	A	M	J	J	A	S	O	N	D
1												
2												
3												
4												
5												
6												
7												
8												
9												
10												
11												
12												
13												
14												
15												
16												
17												
18												
19												
20												
21												
22												
23												
24												
25												
26												
27												
28												
29												
30												
31												

KEYS

- ☐ AMAZING
- ☐ GOOD
- ☐ PRODUCTIVE
- ☐ AVERAGE
- ☐ RELAXED
- ☐ EXHAUSTED
- ☐ DEPRESSED
- ☐ BORED
- ☐ SICK

NOTES

____
____
____
____
____
____
____
____
____
____

BRAIN DUMP

PET CARE CHART

CHORES	Mon	Tue	Wed	Thu	Fri	Sat	Sun
Feed Pet							
Water Pet							

EXTRA STUFF I DID FOR MY PET TODAY

REWARD STICKERS

30 DAY CHALLENGE

Challenge Name:

Start Date:

End Date:

Day 1	Day 2	Day 3	Day 4	Day 5
Day 6	Day 7	Day 8	Day 9	Day 10
Day 11	Day 12	Day 13	Day 14	Day 15
Day 16	Day 17	Day 18	Day 19	Day 20
Day 21	Day 22	Day 23	Day 24	Day 25
Day 26	Day 27	Day 28	Day 29	Day 30

WHAT I AM GRATEFUL FOR?

CHORE CHART

Morning Tasks	Sun	Mon	Tue	Wed	Thu	Fri	Sat

Evening Tasks	Sun	Mon	Tue	Wed	Thu	Fri	Sat

DAILY CHORE CHART

Daily Tasks	Sun	Mon	Tue	Wed	Thu	Fri	Sat

Notes

WEEKLY CHORE CHART

ZONE	CHORES
Floors	
Bathroom	
Kitchen	
Bedroom 1	
Bedroom 2	
Master's	

CLEANING TASKS

Date	Tasks	Instructions

KIDS DAILY MEALS

| Monday | Tuesday | Wednesday |

| Thursday | Friday | Saturday |

Sunday

Note

DAILY MEAL PLANNER

Breakfast

Snacks

Lunch

Notes

Dinner

Fruits

Vegetables

MEAL PLANNER

Monday	Tuesday	Wednesday	Thursday	Friday	Saturday	Sunday

MEAL TRACKER

	Breakfast	Lunch	Dinner	Snack
Monday				
Tuesday				
Wednesday				
Thursday				
Friday				
Saturday				
Sunday				

STUDY PLANNER

Subject:

M T W T F S S

Books/Curriculum

Projects

Activity/Field Trip

Website

Notes

STUDY TASK LIST

Subject:

Subject:

Subject:

Subject:

Subject:

Subject:

GRADE TRACKER

Class: _______________________

Date	Assignment	Your Source	Point Possible

HOMEWORK TRACKER

Month:

Monday	Tuesday	Wednesday	Thursday	Friday

SLEEP TRACKER

DATE	HOURS OF SLEEP												ENERGY
DAY	1	2	3	4	5	6	7	8	9	10	11	12	★ ★ ★ ★ ★
													☆ ☆ ☆ ☆ ☆
													☆ ☆ ☆ ☆ ☆
													☆ ☆ ☆ ☆ ☆
													☆ ☆ ☆ ☆ ☆
													☆ ☆ ☆ ☆ ☆
													☆ ☆ ☆ ☆ ☆
													☆ ☆ ☆ ☆ ☆
													☆ ☆ ☆ ☆ ☆
													☆ ☆ ☆ ☆ ☆
													☆ ☆ ☆ ☆ ☆
													☆ ☆ ☆ ☆ ☆
													☆ ☆ ☆ ☆ ☆
													☆ ☆ ☆ ☆ ☆
													☆ ☆ ☆ ☆ ☆
													☆ ☆ ☆ ☆ ☆
													☆ ☆ ☆ ☆ ☆
													☆ ☆ ☆ ☆ ☆
													☆ ☆ ☆ ☆ ☆
													☆ ☆ ☆ ☆ ☆
													☆ ☆ ☆ ☆ ☆
													☆ ☆ ☆ ☆ ☆
													☆ ☆ ☆ ☆ ☆
													☆ ☆ ☆ ☆ ☆
													☆ ☆ ☆ ☆ ☆
													☆ ☆ ☆ ☆ ☆
													☆ ☆ ☆ ☆ ☆
													☆ ☆ ☆ ☆ ☆
													☆ ☆ ☆ ☆ ☆
													☆ ☆ ☆ ☆ ☆
													☆ ☆ ☆ ☆ ☆

SAVINGS TRACKER

SAVING FOR

START DATE

AMOUNT

GOAL DATE

BOOK WISHLIST

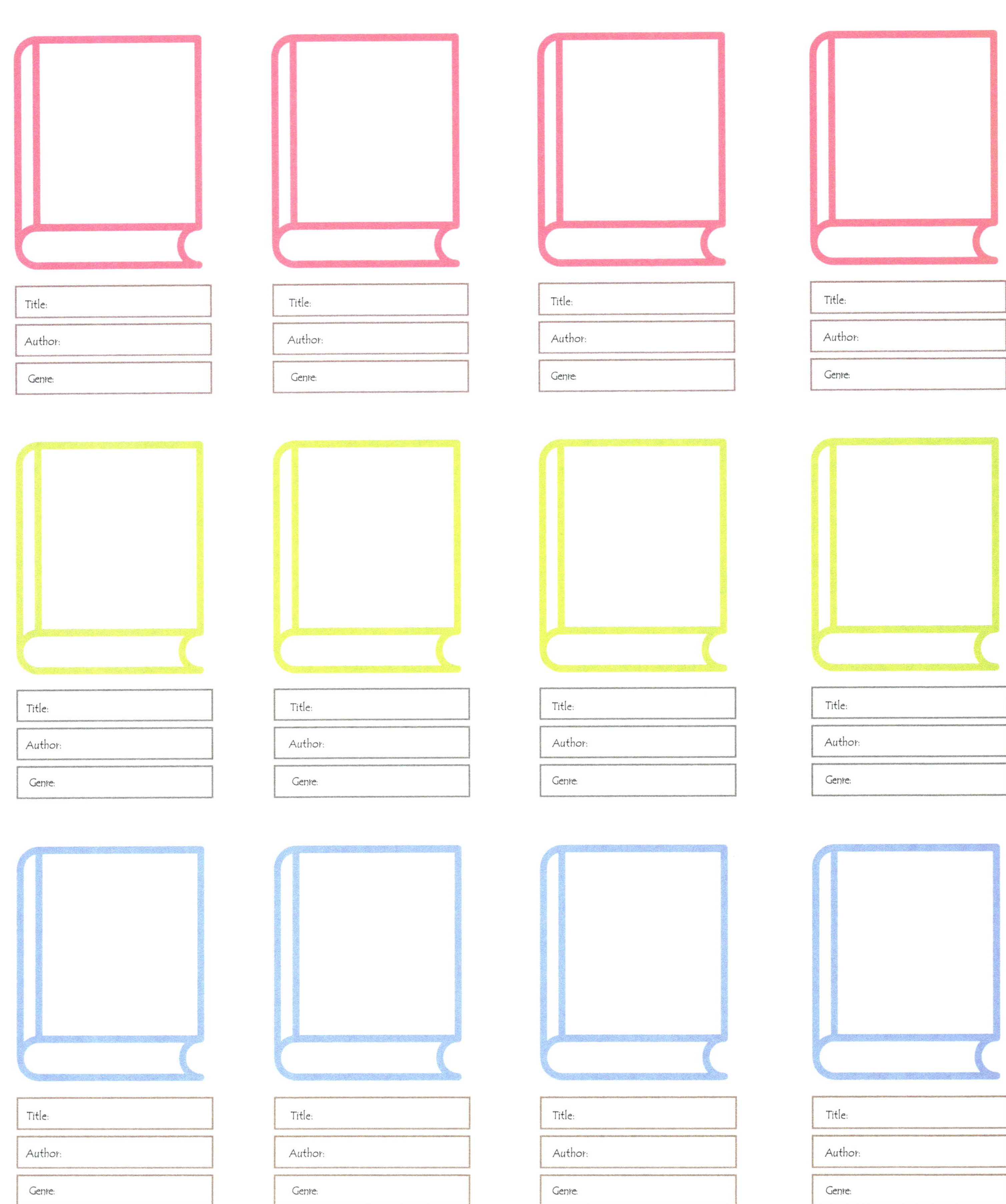

BOOK TRACKER

TITLE	AUTHOR	RATING
		☆ ☆ ☆ ☆ ☆
		☆ ☆ ☆ ☆ ☆
		☆ ☆ ☆ ☆ ☆
		☆ ☆ ☆ ☆ ☆
		☆ ☆ ☆ ☆ ☆
		☆ ☆ ☆ ☆ ☆
		☆ ☆ ☆ ☆ ☆
		☆ ☆ ☆ ☆ ☆
		☆ ☆ ☆ ☆ ☆
		☆ ☆ ☆ ☆ ☆
		☆ ☆ ☆ ☆ ☆
		☆ ☆ ☆ ☆ ☆
		☆ ☆ ☆ ☆ ☆
		☆ ☆ ☆ ☆ ☆
		☆ ☆ ☆ ☆ ☆
		☆ ☆ ☆ ☆ ☆
		☆ ☆ ☆ ☆ ☆

BOOK REVIEW

Title:

Author:

Genre:

Date Published:

#of Page:

Start Date:

End Date:

HABIT TRACKER

HABITS	SUN	MON	TUE	WED	THU	FRI	SAT
________							
________							
________							
________							
________							
________							
________							
________							
________							
________							
________							
________							

HABIT TRACKER

HABITS	Mon	Tue	Wed	Thu	Fri	Sat	Sun
Drink water after waking up							
Do a small exercise							
Take a shower							
Eat a healthy breakfast							
Hangout with friends							
Do house chores							
Write in my journal							
Cook dinner							
Read my favorite book							
Do skincare routine							

REWARD OF THE MONTH

SELF-REFLECTION NOTE

HOLIDAY MEMORIES

Day 1

Day 2

Day 3

HOLIDAY PLANNER

Date :
____

Packing List

Activity list

Places To Go

Note

YEAR AT GLANCE

January	**February**	**March**
April	**May**	**June**
July	**August**	**September**
October	**November**	**December**

FAVORITE QUOTES

TO DO LIST

Must Do	Should Do
Could Do	If Have Time

EXPENSE TRACKER

ITEM	COST	PRICE

DOCTORS APPOINTMENT

Date :   Time :

PATIENT :   AGE :

HOSPITAL :   HEIGHT :

DOCTOR :   WEIGHT :

CONTACT INFO :   HEART RATE :

LOCATION :   BLOOD PRESSURE :

REASON FOR VISIT

DOCTORS COMMENTS

PRESCRIPTION & INSTRUCTIONS

FOLLOW UP CHECKUP   DATE :   TIME :

Creativity 30 DAY CHALLENGE

Tidy your workspace	Take a different route	Read a nonfiction book	Start a dream journal	Goto bed earlier
Watch film	Try a new cuisine	Listen to classical music	Plan a holiday	Practice yoga
Try a DIY Project	Watch the sunrise	No phone day	Self care day	Try a DIY Project
Stretch	Read a book	Explore a new city	Go outside your comfort zone	Make moodboard
Goto bed earlier	Start a new hobby	Make time for exercise	Read a newspaper	Watch the sunset
Visit a museum	Learn a new skill	Create your ideal future	Do nothing	Go outside

Let's Draw!
30 DAY CHALLENGE

Flowers	Kites in the Sky	Butterflies	Teddy Bears	Superheroes
Robots and Machines	Doodle Monsters	Favorite Food	Favorite Animals	Pirate Treasure Map
Candy Land	Hot Air Balloon	My Dream Superhero	My Ideal Treehouse	My Perfect Playground
Superhero Pets	Dreamy Skies	Whimsical Hats	Magical Forest Creatures	Artistic Patterns
Friendly Monsters	Create Your Planet	A Day at the Beach	Sunset	Sunrise
Musical Instruments	Outer Space	Fantasy Creatures	Underwater World	Enchanted Forest

IMPORTANT NOTES

DOTTED NOTES

YOUR 30 DAY CHALLENGE

Let's Draw!

This section is your space to unleash creativity and have fun through drawing.

Let's explore and create together!

Let's Draw!

This section is your space to unleash creativity and have fun through drawing.

Let's explore and create together!

Let's Draw!

This section is your space to unleash creativity and have fun through drawing.

Let's explore and create together!

Let's Draw!

This section is your space to unleash creativity and have fun through drawing.

Let's explore and create together!

You're amazing – look at everything you've accomplished!

As you wrap up today's journey in your planner, take a moment to celebrate all the hard work you put in. Every task, every step, big or small, brings you closer to your goals, and you're doing an incredible job! Remember, tomorrow is a new day filled with fresh chances to learn, grow, and shine even brighter.

Rest up, recharge, and get ready to tackle new adventures tomorrow – the world is lucky to have someone as awesome as you!